The Law of Ueki 3

うえきの法則

The Law of Ueki 3

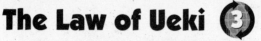

STORY AND ART BY TSUBASA FUKUCHI

VIZ Media Edition

Translation & Adaptation/Yoshiko Tokuhara and Filomila Papakonstantinou
Touch-up Art & Lettering/Avril Averill
Cover Design & Graphic Layout/Amy Martin
Editor/Andy Nakatani

Managing Editor/Annette Roman
Editorial Director/Elizabeth Kawasaki
Editor in Chief/Alvin Lu
Sr. Director of Acquisitions/Rika Inouye
Sr. VP of Marketing/Liza Coppola
Exec. VP of Sales & Marketing/John Easum
Publisher/Hyoe Narita

Printed in the U.S.A.

Published by VIZ Media, LLC
P.O. Box 77010
San Francisco, CA 94107

VIZ Media Edition
10 9 8 7 6 5 4 3 2 1
First printing, December 2006

www.viz.com

store.viz.com

The Law of Ueki™

うえきの法則

3

福地 翼

TSUBASA FUKUCHI PRESENTS

The Characters in The Law of Ueki

Character Profiles The Law of Ueki

Kosuke Ueki

A first-year student at Hinokuni Junior High. He's been given the power to transform trash into trees.

Mr. Kobayashi (Mr. K)

A teacher at Hinokuni Junior High who also happens to be one of the King candidates. He gave Ueki the power to turn trash into trees.

Ai Mori

Ueki's classmate. She's curious about Ueki's power and decides to protect Ueki's talents.

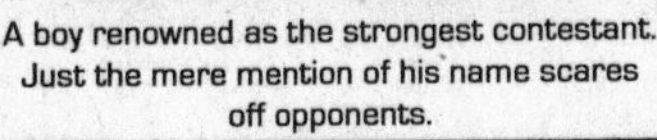

A boy renowned as the strongest contestant. Just the mere mention of his name scares off opponents.

A 14-year old boy who loves hip hop. He was defeated by Robert and lost his power.

The Story of The Law of Ueki

The Story Thus Far The Law of Ueki

IN A WORLD OF POWERFUL CELESTIAL BEINGS, AN EPIC CONTEST IS BEING HELD TO SELECT THE NEXT KING! EACH CELESTIAL SELECTS A KID IN JUNIOR HIGH TO BE HIS CHAMPION AND GRANTS HIM A SPECIAL POWER. THE KIDS BATTLE IT OUT, AND THE LOSERS ARE ELIMINATED. IF THE KIDS USE THEIR POWERS TO HURT A NON-COMBATANT, THEY LOSE ONE OF THEIR TALENTS. WHEN THEY LOSE ALL THEIR TALENTS, THEY VANISH! THE GRAND PRIZE FOR THE ULTIMATE WINNER OF THE TOURNAMENT IS THE TALENT OF BLANK WHERE THE WINNER CAN FILL IN THE BLANK WITH ANY TALENT OF HIS CHOOSING.

KOSUKE UEKI, A FIRST-YEAR STUDENT AT HINOKUNI JUNIOR HIGH, HAS BEEN UNWITTINGLY ENTERED INTO THE TOURNAMENT BY HIS HOMEROOM TEACHER, MR. K. GRANTED THE POWER TO TURN TRASH INTO TREES, UEKI HAS A DISADVANTAGE TO OVERCOME—FOR SOME REASON, MR. K WANTS TO KEEP UEKI IN THE DARK ABOUT THE RULES OF THE GAME. ALSO, IT SEEMS UEKI COULD CARE LESS ABOUT WINNING OR LOSING. IF SOMETHING IRRITATES HIM, THEN THERE'S NO STOPPING HIM—EVEN IF IT MEANS LOSING ONE OF HIS PRECIOUS TALENTS. FORTUNATELY, UEKI'S CLASSMATE, AI MORI, HAS SWORN TO PROTECT UEKI.

UEKI HAS HAD A WINNING STREAK SO FAR, DEFEATING TAIRA, ADACHI AND HOLDING HIS OWN AGAINST THE POWERFUL LI HO. WITH AI'S HELP, HE FINDS OUT ABOUT THE LAW OF UEKI, ACCORDING TO WHICH HE GAINS A NEW TALENT EVERY TIME HE DEFEATS AN OPPONENT. UEKI ALSO GOES UP AGAINST B.J., THE HIP HOPPER WITH A PENCHANT FOR LYING. UEKI ENJOYS HIS FIGHT WITH B.J. AND SHOWS HIM MERCY, BUT B.J. IS LATER BRUTALLY BEATEN BY ROBERT, THE STRONGEST CONTESTANT OF THE ENTIRE TOURNAMENT.

Table of Contents

Chapter 19
Nice to Meet You!

Hinokuni Junior High School

...

HALF A YEAR HAS ALREADY GONE-BY SINCE I MET UEKI...
WHO ARE YOU, POPS?
WHAT DO YOU MEAN POPS? I'M ONLY 30 YEARS OLD.

LET ME TELL YOU WHO I REALLY AM...
I'M A CELESTIAL FROM THE CELESTIAL WORLD!
DADUM
SHUF SHUF SHUF
GO ON BACK TO THE CELESTIAL WORLD THEN.
I'm busy with errands.
SO COLD !!!

HEH HEH...
UEKI COULD CARE LESS ABOUT ME BEING A CELESTIAL.

EVEN WHEN HE ENTERED JUNIOR HIGH...
CHATTER CHATTER
HMM?

HEY! HOW HAVE YOU BEEN?
WELL, YOU HAVEN'T USED YOUR POWER TO HURT ANYONE JUST LIKE YOU PROMISED.

NICE TO MEET YOU. I'M KOSUKE UEKI.
BOW
BUT WE'VE ALREADY...
hey!
HE DIDN'T REMEMBER ME AT ALL...

1-C

ZHOOP
BUT...
HELLO! Take your seats!

I'VE BEEN WATCHING UEKI THESE SIX MONTHS.
DADOOM
OKAY, TIME FOR A HISTORY POP QUIZ!!
I WANT TO FIND OUT WHETHER OR NOT TRUE JUSTICE STILL EXISTS IN THIS WORLD.
WHAT?!

I'VE WITNESSED QUITE A FEW INSTANCES OF YOUR MORALS AND SENSE OF JUSTICE...

ZRAKKT

DING DONG DING DONG
TIME'S UP!!
No!!!
Hand in your tests!

How'd you do?
Not too bad!
It was tough...
HEY, UEKI!
To be honest...

COME TO THE FACULTY ROOM AFTER SCHOOL.
Mori, you too!
CHATTER
!
CHATTER
MRMR
MRMR

I ENTERED UEKI INTO THE BATTLE TOURNAMENT, BECAUSE I WANTED TO CONTINUE TESTING HIS SENSE OF JUSTICE...
DOES IT MEAN I MIGHT FLUNK BECAUSE MY SCORES ARE TOO LOW?!
Why'd he call me too?!
GASP

THERE'S NO NEED TO TEST UEKI ANYMORE...

Faculty

STAY AWAY FROM ROBERT HAYDN.

WAIT...

HOLD ON. WHAT ARE YOU TALKING ABOUT?!
ROBERT?

ROBERT THAT HIP HOP GUY?!
Yay!!
THAT KID WAS JUST USING ROBERT HAYDN'S NAME.

THAT KID...
B.J.?
YES.

B.J. WAS DEFEATED.
HE WAS BADLY HURT. IT'LL TAKE AT LEAST THREE MONTHS FOR HIM TO RECOVER.
He's lucky to be alive.

...

WHAT? HE WAS JUST AN IMPOSTOR...
...POSING AS ROBERT?
PHEW

YOU MEAN AFTER FIGHTING WITH UEKI, B.J. WAS DEFEATED BY THE REAL ROBERT?
BUMMER...

GRAAHH
!

I KNOW IT'S HARD TO ACCEPT, BUT YOU DON'T STAND A CHANCE AGAINST AN OPPONENT LIKE HIM.

DON'T EVEN THINK ABOUT GETTING REVENGE FOR B.J.

DOOM

HE'LL **KILL** YOU!

B.J. SURVIVED, DIDN'T HE?
WHAT'S THE PROBLEM THEN?
DA DOOM

I SEE.

BESIDES, I DON'T EVEN KNOW WHERE THIS ROBERT IS.
HA HA HA! THAT'S RIGHT!
UMM...

Okay! LET'S GO HOME.
ZHOOP
OF COURSE.
THAT B.J. GUY WAS AN ENEMY...

THERE'S NO REASON TO GET REVENGE FOR HIM...
RIGHT, UEKI?

UEKI...

FWP
FLOP

?

Dear Kosuke Ueki,
Nice to meet you. My name is Robert Haydn. I am a second-year Junior High student.
SHRSH

I've heard a lot about you.
I would like to fight you.
Midnight, tonight.
FWP FWP

I'll be waiting for you at the Park.
OKAY!
DASH

HMM?

THERE YOU ARE!

I KNEW YOU'D GO!!

DA DUM

UEKI...
SO, YOU'RE GOING...

THE PARK

NOBODY'S HERE.
ARE YOU SURE THIS IS THE RIGHT PLACE?
...
DESERTED

SEE? THAT LETTER WAS JUST A PRANK!!
OF COURSE! IT MUST BE A TRICK OF MR. K'S! HE'S JUST KIDDING AROUND!!
THERE'S STILL A MINUTE TO GO.
HE WON'T COME!
LET'S GO HOME!! PLEASE?

YOU, IDIOT!! EVEN MR. K SAID THIS ROBERT GUY IS SOMEONE YOU SHOULD STAY AWAY FROM!!!
HE MUST BE A REAL MONSTER!!!

FFF FFFT

WHAT?

SOAP BUBBLES...
WHERE'D THEY COME FROM?

ARE YOU UEKI?
FWP

NICE
TO
FINALLY
MEET
YOU!

Chapter 20
Red and Blue

!!

AT LAST, WE MEET!
UEKI...

MY NAME IS ROBERT HAYDN.

...

HE'S FLOATING ?!!
What's going on?!

WHAT ?

ROBERT...
!

B.J. WAS DEFEATED BY ROBERT HAYDN.
HE WAS BADLY HURT. IT'LL TAKE AT LEAST THREE MONTHS FOR HIM TO RECOVER.

SO...
YOU'RE ROBERT HAYDN.

STOP FLOATING AND COME DOWN !!!
DADOOM
DOES UEKI EVEN REALIZE HOW WEIRD IT IS TO BE FLOATING IN MID-AIR ?!!

KER POP

STOMP

!!!

I GUESSED RIGHT... HE'S USING THE BLUE SOAP BUBBLES TO FLOAT.
ARE SOAP BUBBLES HIS POWER ?!

IT WAS YOU, RIGHT?

HIP HOP IS GREAT, DON'T YOU THINK?

DADOOM

MY NAME IS ROBERT HAYDN!!

AREN'T YOU B.J.?

CHECK IT CHECK IT OUT.

HEY YO, CHECK IT OUT.

YOU BEAT B.J.?

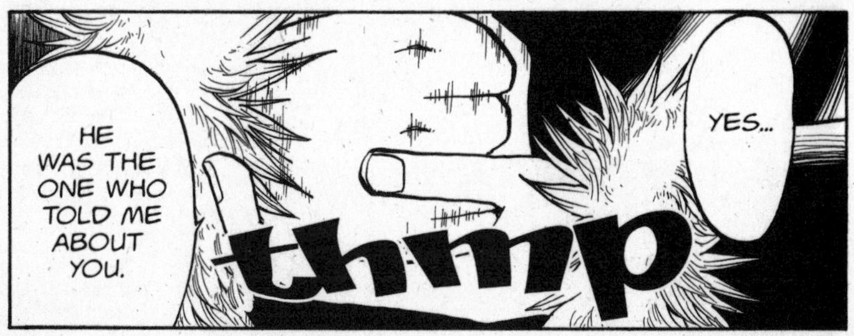

THAT'S RIGHT.

AND IT WAS MUCH TOO EASY TO BEAT HIM, NO FUN AT ALL.

!!!
UEKI!! STOP...
NO WAY...
HE'S REALLY ANGRY...
CLENCH
ALL THIS IS ABOUT THAT B.J. GUY?
FSSHAAA
I SEE.
ZWAP

THUMK

?!
THE TREE GOT AS HEAVY AS LEAD...

CREAAK

WHAT... WAS THAT?
THE TREE WAS PULLED TO THE GROUND JUST BEFORE HITTING HIM!!

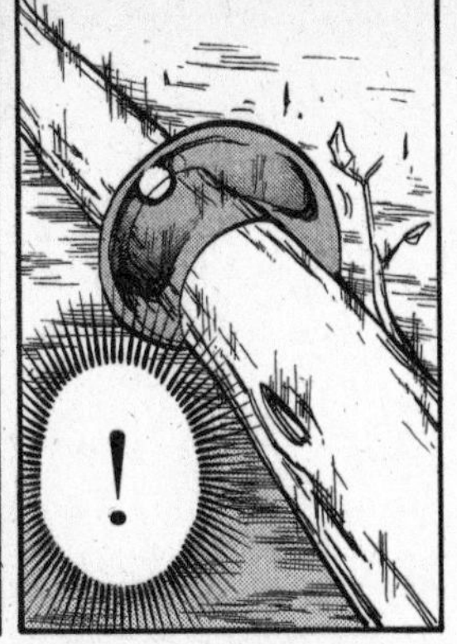
!

NOW HE'S USING SOME KIND OF RED BUBBLE ?!
WHAT SORT OF POWER IS THIS ?!!

!
OKAY...

FSSH AAA

TAKE THIS!
FSHOOOOOM
!!!

Whhmm mmm
PHFT
PLOP
PLOOF
PWOF
NOW A BLUE BUBBLE !!
TWANG

TUP
WHAT A SHAME...
IS THIS ALL YOU'VE GOT?

!!

DASH
UEKI ?!

PADAPADAPADA
HMM ?
PADAPA

FWIP
FSSHAA
FSSHAA

Trash

KLANG

DA
DOOM
SQUIRCH
!
SQUIRCH
SQUIRCH
AS LONG AS YOUR ARMS AND LEGS ARE TIED...
...YOU CAN'T MAKE THOSE STRANGE BUBBLES!
FZ
ZASH

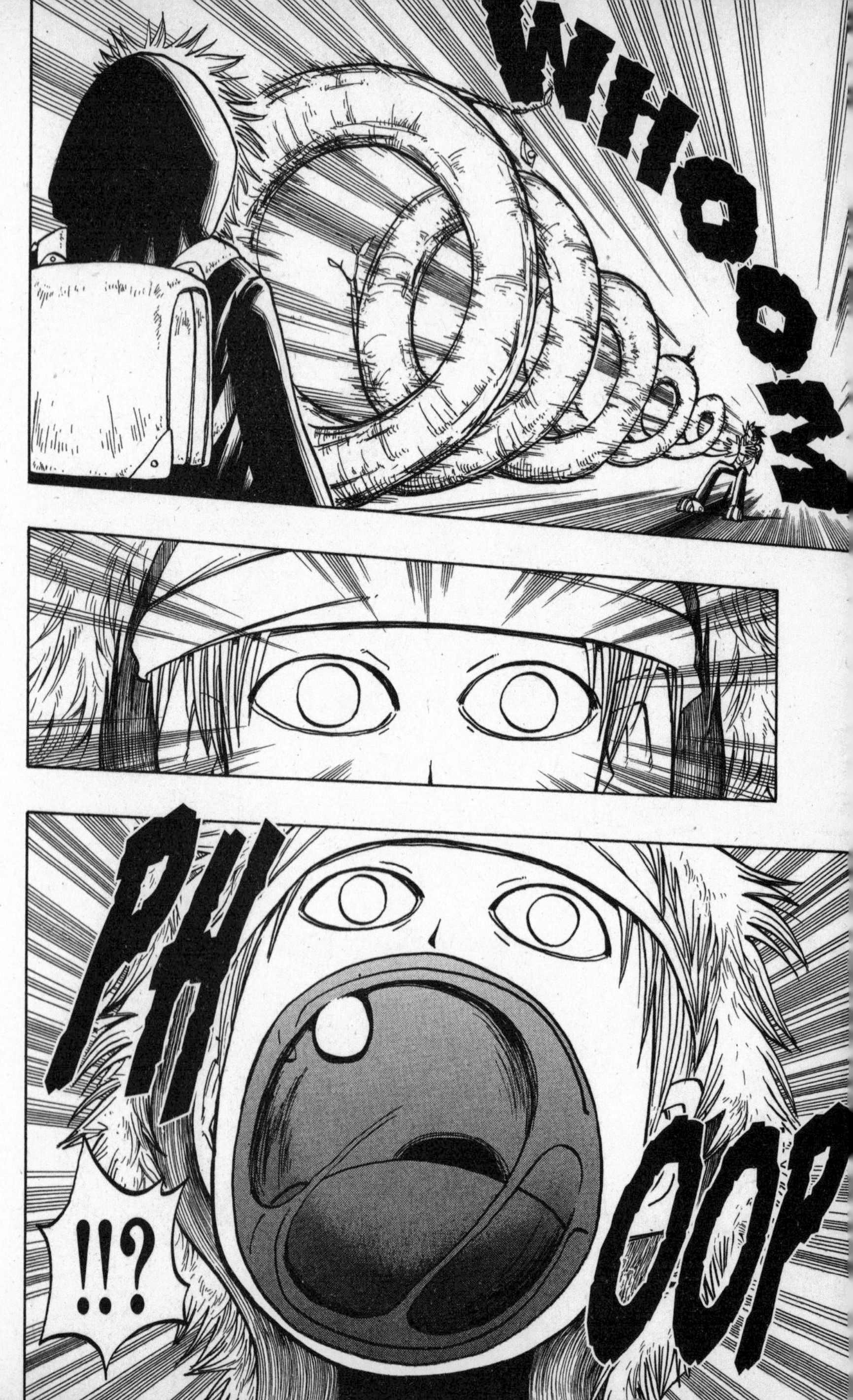
WHOOOM
!!?
PHOOOP

!!
YIKES !!!

ANOTHER RED ONE!!

THUMK

!?
THUD
DOOM

FFF FFT
FWIP
HMM?
!!?

FFFT

I WAS RIGHT! THOSE SOAP BUBBLES...

THE RED ONES MAKE OBJECTS HEAVY AND THE BLUE ONES MAKE THEM LIGHT!!

!

POP

HUH
?

Chapter 21
A Special Moment

WOW
THERE HE GOES.

UEKI!!

WAAH...
AAAAHHH!!!

WHAT ARE YOU DOING?! HE WON'T SURVIVE IF HE FALLS FROM THAT HEIGHT...!!!
FWOOSH
AHA HA HA HA HA!!
SAVE HIM!!
DO SOME-THING!!

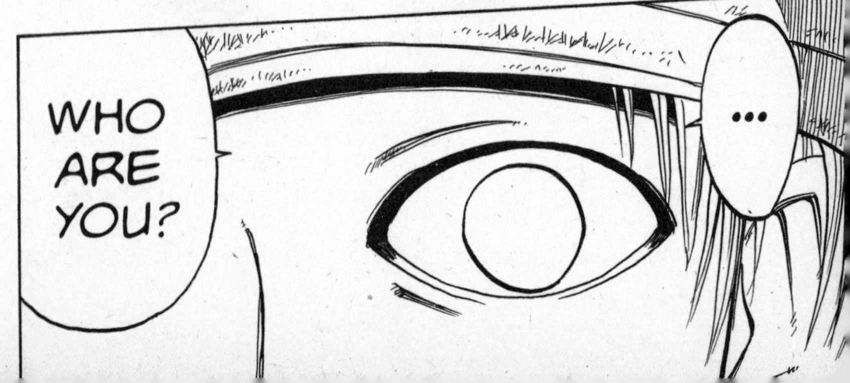

PLOUFF
!!?

A BLUE BUBBLE!!
THIS MAKES OBJECTS LIGHT?!!
FFFT

SEE?
IT WON'T BE LONG NOW.

!!
VWSHHH
SHM

THEY SAY...

DEATH IS ABSOLUTE NOTHINGNESS.

SHWOOM

TAK

!!?

FWIP

KRAKK
KRAKK
KRAKK
GOT IT!! UEKI WANTS TO...
...BREAK HIS FALL WITH THE BRANCHES!!

OH NO, YOU DON'T!
PLOOP

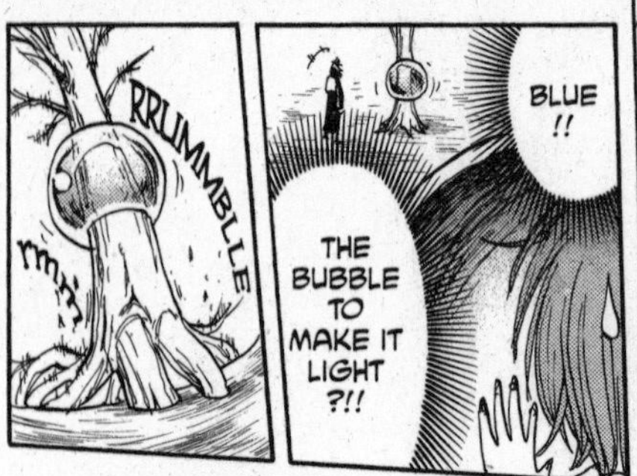
BLUE !!
THE BUBBLE TO MAKE IT LIGHT ?!!
RRUMMBLLE

!!!

KREE

VOOM

YOU'RE OUT OF TRASH, AREN'T YOU?

STOP FIGHTING AND JUST DIE!

WAAAAAHHHH!!!

UEKI!!!

ACCORDING TO THE RULES, IF I HELP UEKI, I WILL BE SENT TO THE UNDERWORLD...
I FEEL BAD, BUT I CAN'T HELP HIM.

BUT, UEKI...
YOU FOUGHT BRAVELY AGAINST AN OPPONENT YOU HAD NO CHANCE OF DEFEATING...

ALL JUST FOR THAT B.J. GUY...
BECAUSE B.J. WAS BRUTALLY BEATEN BY ROBERT!

AND THEN TOO.

EVEN THEN!

YOU'VE REMAINED FAITHFUL TO YOUR OWN SENSE OF JUSTICE!

AND THE ONES WHO MET YOU...
I WILL BECOME STRONG TO PROTECT UEKI!!!
OKAY THEN...
I WILL BE UEKI'S SHIELD.
YOU'LL SEE, I'LL NEVER LOSE TO HIM!!
LET'S HAVE A FIGHT AGAIN SOME-DAY!
KOSUKE UEKI!!

EACH AND EVERY ONE...

I WARNED YOU TO STAY AWAY FROM ROBERT HAYDN...
BUT YOU STILL CHOSE YOUR JUSTICE.

I ALWAYS THOUGHT YOU WERE A FOOL, BUT...
...I DIDN'T KNOW YOU WERE THIS FOOLISH.

...ALL OF THEM WERE INFLUENCED BY YOU, UEKI!!

I WILL WATCH OVER YOU TILL THE END.
UEKI...

I CAN ASSURE YOU THAT TO THE VERY END...
...YOU WERE A RIGHTEOUS FOOL...
LOOK!!
NOT LONG NOW!!
!!

AHHHHHHH!!!

DARN IT!! DARN IT!! DARN IT !!!!!

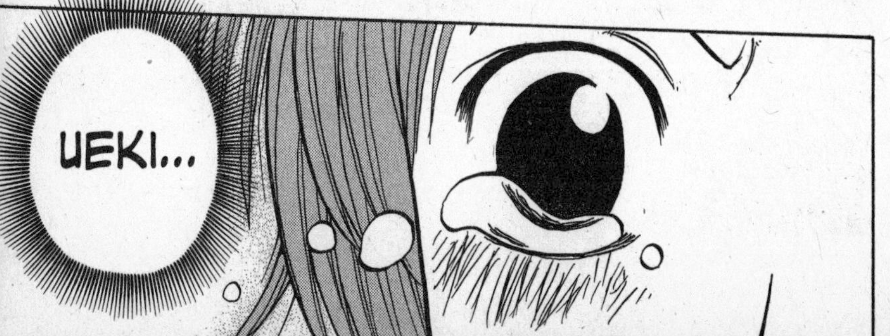

SWO

IF UEKI IS A FOOL...
THEN I AM...
I AM THE KING OF FOOLS.

Chapter 22 True Encounter

WHAT WERE YOU THINKING?

REALLY...

TH UD

UNGH.

MR. K !!!

Chapter 22
True Encounter

WELL DONE!! NICE CATCH!!

YOU CAN BE USEFUL SOMETIMES!!

ONLY SOMETIMES, HUH?

...

...

MR. K!!

BE USEFUL ONE MORE TIME AND GET ME OUT OF THIS!!

HEY! WHAT'S GOING ON ?!!
bwam
bwam
GET ME OUT OF THIS!! HEY!!
SHUT UP.

DO YOU WANT TO BE DRAGGED DOWN WITH ME?
WHAT ?
KEEP QUIET AND STAY AWAY!

YOU TOO, UEKI.
GRAB
KRAKK
HUH ?

WHOOSH
KRAKK
!!!

SKREEE
WHAT THE ...?

CHOOM
!!!

A KING CANDIDATE IS FORBIDDEN TO HELP HIS STUDENT DURING A BATTLE UNDER ANY CIRCUMSTANCES.

IF HE BREAKS THE RULE, THE KING CANDIDATE WILL BE SENT TO THE UNDERWORLD!

!!

FOR...
...ME?

UEKI...
I'VE BEEN HIDING THIS FROM YOU, BUT...
SHOOOOOOF
!
...FOR THE PAST SIX MONTHS I'VE BEEN TESTING YOUR SENSE OF JUSTICE.

I RE-MEMBER THAT DAY I FIRST SAW YOU, IT WAS SNOWING.
!

IT WAS ABOUT A YEAR AFTER I'D COME DOWN TO THIS WORLD.

SOME PRIMARY SCHOOL KIDS WERE ON THEIR WAY HOME...
Wow, what's this?
A puppy! It's so cute!!
OWOOO
WHEN THEY FOUND AN ABANDONED DOG COVERED IN MUD.

JUST ONE...

...FOOLISH BOY.

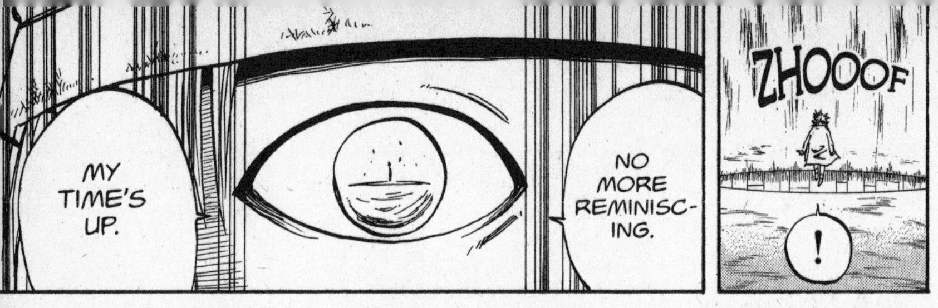
ZHOOOF
!
NO MORE REMINISC-ING.
MY TIME'S UP.

ZHOOOOFF
!
AT THAT MOMENT... I COULD NOT HELP THINKING...
SHOOOOOF
THAT I WANTED TO WATCH YOUR SENSE OF JUSTICE IN ACTION.

SORRY... FOR PUTTING YOU TO THE TEST...
SHOOOOOOF
YOU'RE WRONG!
?

THAT WASN'T THE FIRST TIME WE MET!
IT WAS WAY BEFORE THAT!

WHAT?
?

ABOUT A YEAR AGO...
I WAS PLAYING WITH MY FRIENDS ON THE ROOFTOP OF SOME BUILDING...
I WAS SHOWING OFF WHAT GOOD BALANCE I HAD, AND I WAS WALKING ON THE EDGE OF THE ROOFTOP WHEN I SLIPPED!!

?

I THOUGHT THAT WAS IT.
THOUGHT I WAS DEAD!

MAYBE YOU FORGOT, BUT...
...YOU SAVED ME!!

IT WAS THAT MOMENT THAT I DECIDED TO BECOME SOMEONE WHO WOULD SACRIFICE HIMSELF FOR OTHERS...

Jumping off a roof? What were you thinking?

I WANTED TO BECOME LIKE YOU, THE PERSON WHO SAVED ME!!!

DO WHATEVER YOU WANT !!!
THIS IS YOUR LIFE !!!

RRROOOOOOOSHH
SHOOOOOFF

SQUEEFROP
SSSHOOOOF

ZPFT

PHEW.
FWIP

THAT MEDDLER IS GONE AT LAST!

HA HA. QUIT THE BATTLE? THERE'S NO NEED FOR THAT SINCE YOU ARE GOING TO DIE TODAY.
YOU'LL HAVE FUN IN THE UNDER-WORLD. ♡

YOU THINK SO?

GRAB
THEN WHY DON'T YOU JOIN ME?
KRKK
!!!!!
WHAT...

AHHHHHHHHHHHH?!!

THUD
OUCH!

THAT HURT.
HUH...

MR...
MR. K?

FWOOOSH
...

HUH?

EVER SINCE I FOUND OUT ABOUT UEKI'S POWER, IT'S BEEN...
...ONE STRANGE THING AFTER ANOTHER, BUT...

NOW THAT MR. K IS GONE...
IT ALL FEELS JUST LIKE A DREAM.

STARE
BUT...

HE'S THE SAME AS EVER.
WHERE DID THEY GO ?!
FWIP
WILL THEY COME OUT AGAIN ?!
FWIP

I DON'T REALLY UNDERSTAND WHAT HAPPENED, BUT...
Hey...

EVERYTHING IS OVER NOW...
HEY, UEKI, LET'S GO HOME!
drag drag drag
MR. K...
STOMP STOMP STOMP

WE CAN FINALLY GO BACK TO OUR ORDINARY CAREFREE LIVES.

OR SO I THOUGHT...

Hey!! Get on your feet and walk!!

SCHNORR

Chapter 23 The Tree Devil

NOT AGAIN... A DOG MUST HAVE DUG IT UP.

...

FWSH
!

FWIP
FWIP

No matter how hard the brave warrior looked for the Tree Devil, he could not find him.
That was because...
The Brave Warrior and the Tree Devil
The Brave Warrior and t

UNBELIEVABLE!! THE TREE DEVIL TOOK HUMAN FORM...
...IN ORDER TO CONQUER EARTH!!!

ULP
THE TREE DEVIL...

Fukus
Hibi

?

CLENCH

!!?

!!!
IT'S...
PAT

Chapter 23
The Tree Devil
Waaaah!
THE TREE DEVIL !!!
PAT

Hinokuni Junior High School
UEKI...
I'LL GIVE YOU SOME-THING...
THE POWER THAT MR. K GAVE ME...
...
I STILL HAVE THE POWER.
THE POWER TO TRANSFORM TRASH...
...INTO TREES!!!

IT SEEMS THAT THERE ARE OTHER PEOPLE BESIDES ME WHO HAVE DIFFERENT POWERS IN THIS WORLD...
AND THEY'RE FIGHTING FOR SOMETHING CALLED THE TALENT OF BLANK.

MESSY

FWAP

WHRRR
TCHAK

SHUNK SHUNK SHUNK
TIDY
What just happened?

1-C
ZHOOP
GOOD MORNING.

HAVE YOU HEARD?!
MR. K WAS SUDDENLY TRANSFERRED TO A DIFFERENT SCHOOL!!
SKWK
NO WAY! HE WAS A COOL TEACHER!!

...
MR. K WAS OUR HOMEROOM TEACHER.

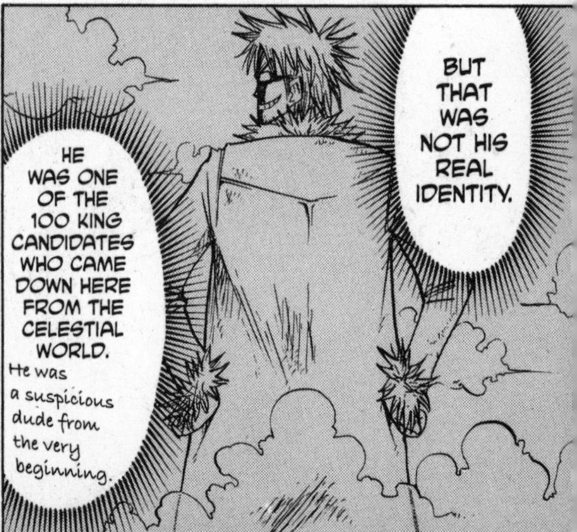
BUT THAT WAS NOT HIS REAL IDENTITY.
HE WAS ONE OF THE 100 KING CANDIDATES WHO CAME DOWN HERE FROM THE CELESTIAL WORLD.
He was a suspicious dude from the very beginning.

HE GAVE ME A WEIRD POWER...
...AND ENROLLED ME IN A STRANGE BATTLE TOURNAMENT WITHOUT ASKING ME...
FWP FWP FWP
...AND THEN...

HE SACRIFICED HIS OWN LIFE...
...TO SAVE MINE!

BUT... WHY DID MR. K...
...SAVE SOME-ONE LIKE ME?

GOOD MORNING.

GOOD MORNING! AI, LOOK, LOOK!
OH TOMO, YOU GOT A NEW HAIR STYLE?
YOU LOOK REALLY NICE! BUT WITH THAT STYLE, YOU'D LOOK PRETTIER IF YOU PARTED YOUR HAIR TO THIS SIDE!
HEY, I SAW A HAIRPIN THAT WOULD GO PERFECT WITH THAT LOOK! I'LL GET IT FOR YOU.
THAT'S AI MORI.
SHE REALLY LIKES TAKING CARE OF PEOPLE.

YOU SAY SOME-THING, UEKI?
NO, NOTHING.
AND SHE'S GOT A KEEN SIXTH SENSE.

UEKI!
I NEED TO TELL YOU SOME-THING.

THE BATTLE IS OVER!

MR. K ISN'T COMING BACK, SO YOU STOP THINKING ABOUT IT.
IT'S ALL OVER NOW.

OH, THE PAIN! THE PAIN!!!
WHAT?! What's wrong?

I'VE GOT A HEAD-ACHE...
I'M LEAVING!
ZHOOP
WHERE ARE YOU GOING?! What headache? You were holding your tummy!!

UE...
Hey!
!

UEKI!!!
.....
DASH

1-G
WAIT... NO NEED TO WORRY ABOUT HIM ANYMORE...
EVERY-THING IS OVER...!

...

MR. K...

MR. K ISN'T COMING BACK, SO YOU STOP THINKING ABOUT IT.
I KNOW THAT.

I JUST WANT TO KNOW...

...WHY HE SACRIFICED HIMSELF...
...TO SAVE ME...

TAK
ALSO...

...WHO THE HECK IS THIS KID?
STARE
THE ONE WHO'S BEEN FOLLOWING ME!!!

Tsubame Primary School

1-1

FUKUSUKE IS NOT HERE YET, TEACHER.
I SEE... FUKUSUKE ABSENT...

HE'S IN DISGUISE AS A JUNIOR HIGH SCHOOL STUDENT.
SHUF SHUF SHUF
BUT HE CAN'T DECEIVE ME!!

YOU'RE A TREE DEVIL PLOTTING TO CONQUER THE EARTH!!!
I WILL GET PROOF OF YOUR EVIL DEEDS AND UNMASK YOU!!
Ha ha!

HUH?!!
DASH
HE'S RUNNING AWAY !!!

NO WAY! I WON'T LOSE YOU!!
DASH
I WILL EXPOSE YOU!!

HE IS THE TREE DEVIL...
The Brave Warrior and the Tree Devil
Story & Art Robin Blossom the Third
HE DOES EVIL DEEDS BY CONTROLLING PLANTS!
It true!

WAIT!

WAIT!

...
...
RUNS WHEN CHASED.

HUFF
HUFF
HUFF

I LOST HIM.
BUT IT'S JUST LIKE THE PICTURE BOOK DE-SCRIBES.
HUFF
THE TREE DEVIL RUNS AWAY AS SOON AS HE IS IN DANGER!!
HUFF
HUFF

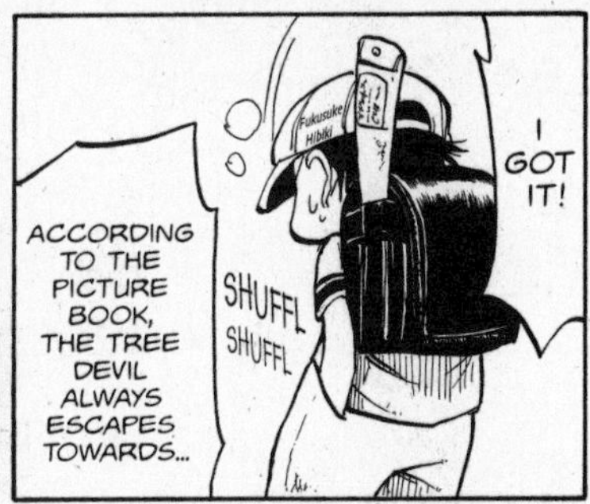
I GOT IT!
Fukusuke Hibiki
SHUFFL
SHUFFL
ACCORDING TO THE PICTURE BOOK, THE TREE DEVIL ALWAYS ESCAPES TOWARDS...

...THE WEST !!
DADUM

WELL...
HUFF HUFF
WHERE IS HE?

AM I SEARCHING IN ALL THE WRONG PLACES?
SIGH...

Fuk
HEY!!!
HMM ?
THERE YOU ARE !!!

SLIP
!!?
GAH...
WAHHHHHH!!!

!!!
WHUMP
?
...
PHEW. What's with you?

I...

FWOP

I HAVE TO FIND OUT!!!

Chapter 24

Mr. K's Last Message

DING
DONG
DING
DONG
UEKI THAT IDIOT...
I'm leaving!!!
Headache!!
DASH
WHY'D HE SKIP CLASS? WHERE'S HE GOING?
!
YIKES
AND WHY AM I STILL WORRYING ABOUT EVERYTHING HE DOES?
No more no more!!

IT'S ALL OVER!!
WITH MR. K GONE...
...I DON'T NEED TO WORRY ABOUT THE BATTLE ANY MORE!!

STOMP STOMP STOMP
IT'S GOT NOTHING TO DO WITH ME!!

STOMP STOMP STOMP
DARN IT!!

YOU JUST WAIT AND SEE, TREE DEVIL!!!
Hmm ?
SOMEDAY I WILL DEFINITELY EXPOSE YOUR TRUE IDENTITY!!!

201
Kobayashi

ENTRY DATE: XX/XX/XX
UEKI FOUND A WALLET AND TOOK IT TO THE POLICE.

ENTRY DATE: XX/XX/XX
XX/XX/XX
UEKI HELPED AN OLD LADY WHO GOT LOST.
UEKI HELPED AN OLD LADY WHO GOT LOST.

ENTRY DATE: XX/XX/XX
UEKI PLANTED A TREE IN A PARK AGAIN.

...
THIS IS ALL ABOUT ME...

MR. K'S DIARY IS FILLED WITH...
...WHAT I'VE BEEN DOING DURING THE LAST FEW MONTHS.

WHY DID MR. K SACRIFICE HIMSELF TO SAVE ME?
I BROKE INTO HIS APARTMENT TO FIND A CLUE WHY HE DID THAT, BUT...
BREAKING AND ENTERING.
NO! THERE MUST BE SOMETHING IN THIS DIARY!!
I'LL READ IT COVER TO COVER TO MAKE SURE I DON'T MISS ANYTHING!!

ENTRY DATE: XX/XX/XX UEKI HURT A NON-COMBATANT WITH HIS POWER FOR THE FIRST TIME.
I REMEMBER THAT!
UEKI LOST HIS TALENT TO BE LIKED BY GIRLS.

EVERY TIME HE HURTS A NON-COMBATANT WITH HIS POWER...
...ONE OF HIS TALENTS WILL DISAPPEAR AS PUNISHMENT.
IT'S THE RULE OF THIS TOURNAMENT.
HE STOPPED BEING LIKED BY GIRLS. SERVES YOU RIGHT, UEKI.
MR. K. WAS ENJOYING THIS.

KAW
KAW

HMM... HE WAS WRITING DOWN EVERYTHING I WAS DOING...
THE ONLY PART I HAVEN'T READ YET IS YESTERDAY'S ENTRY...
MUNCH
MUNCH
Thought it would take a while so he went food shopping.

ENTRY DATE: XX/XX/XX
CLICK CLICK
SUCH A LOVELY DAY.

I WONDER HOW MUCH JUSTICE AND...
...HOW MUCH EVIL EXISTS IN THIS WORLD?
I CANNOT TOLERATE THOSE WHO HAVE NO SENSE OF JUSTICE.

TWITCH
JUSTICE !!!

EVER SINCE I CAME TO THIS WORLD, I'VE MET A VARIETY OF PEOPLE.
BUT NONE OF THEM HAD A TRUE SENSE OF JUSTICE.

I WAS LOSING INTEREST IN SUCH A BORING WORLD.
AND I WAS THINKING OF GOING BACK TO THE CELESTIAL WORLD.
BUT THEN...

...I MET UEKI.
!!!
BABUMP

I COULD HARDLY BELIEVE IT, BUT UEKI'S SENSE OF JUSTICE SEEMED TO BE THE REAL THING.
...NO, IT WASN'T.

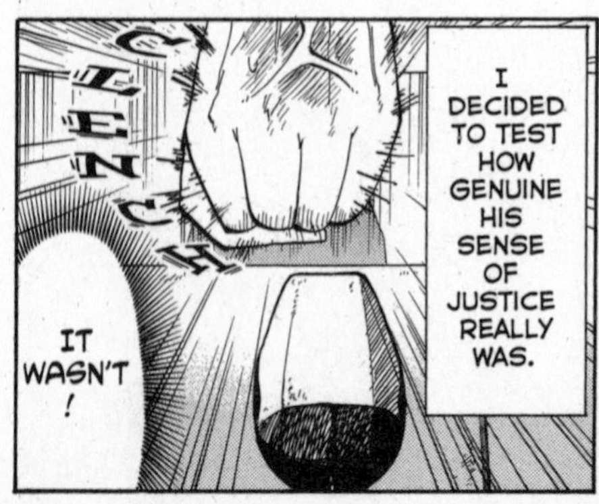
I DECIDED TO TEST HOW GENUINE HIS SENSE OF JUSTICE REALLY WAS.
CLENCH
IT WASN'T!

HIS SENSE OF JUSTICE WAS GENUINE.
IT WAS NOT !!!

I DIDN'T HAVE SUCH A SENSE OF JUSTICE BEFORE I MET YOU!!

I WAS JUST AN ORDINARY KID LIKE ANY OTHER!!

I WANTED TO BECOME THE TYPE OF PERSON WHO CARES ABOUT OTHERS MORE THAN HIMSELF...

MR. K...

I JUST WANTED TO BECOME LIKE YOU !!!

I...
I STARTED HELPING OTHERS JUST LIKE YOU DID!
THAT WAS ALL !!
I WANTED TO BE JUST LIKE YOU !!
THAT'S...
THAT'S WHY THIS ISN'T MY SENSE OF JUSTICE !!

IT'S YOUR SENSE OF JUSTICE!!

BUT...
!
I'M WORRIED ABOUT ONE THING.

THE PRIZE OF THIS TOURNAMENT.

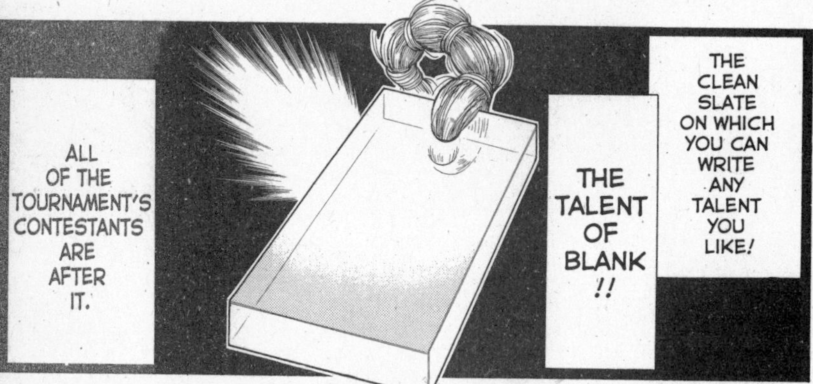
THE CLEAN SLATE ON WHICH YOU CAN WRITE ANY TALENT YOU LIKE!
THE TALENT OF BLANK!!
ALL OF THE TOURNAMENT'S CONTESTANTS ARE AFTER IT.

BUT MOST OF THESE CONTESTANTS HAVE NO SENSE OF JUSTICE WHAT-SO-EVER....
THEY ARE EVIL!!
IF THE TALENT OF BLANK FALLS INTO THEIR HANDS, THIS WORLD WILL BE PLUNGED INTO CHAOS.
BUT WE KING CANDIDATES DON'T HAVE THE RIGHT OR POWER TO PREVENT IT!
THERE'S ONLY ONE PERSON THAT CAN...

...THE KID WHO JOINS THIS TOURNAMENT WHO...
BUT I CAN'T EXPECT UEKI TO DO IT...
...I ONLY WANTED TO CONFIRM WHETHER HIS SENSE OF JUSTICE WAS GENUINE.
...HAS A TRUE SENSE OF JUSTICE!!!
CLICK
POWER
WHIRRR
...

THAT...

...I CAN DO FOR YOU!

I WILL DEFEAT ALL THOSE EVIL GUYS...
...AND WIN THIS TOURNAMENT !!!

DADOOM
MORI?!! WHEN DID YOU--?!

DING DONG

HELLO.

I AM THE NEW KING CANDIDATE!

DING DONG

!!!

BABUMP

HE'S LATE!!
THUMP
WHAT'S WITH THAT NEW KING CANDIDATE?! HE'S THE ONE WHO ASKED US TO MEET HIM!!

Chapter 25
The New Candidate

HE SHOWED UP IN MR. K'S APARTMENT OUT OF THE BLUE AND THEN...
THIS ROOM IS TOO STUFFY.
LET'S MEET THIS SATURDAY AT THREE AT THE CAFETERIA IN FRONT OF THE STATION.
What?

IT'S ALREADY ONE MINUTE TO THREE, AND THERE'S NO SIGN OF HIM!!
SLURP
THERE'S STILL A MINUTE LEFT.
42 SECONDS, TO BE EXACT.
41...
40...
3... 2...
1...
THERE HE IS.

DADOOOM
YES! HERE I AM.
Chapter 25
The New Candidate

I'M HERE TO TAKE OVER FOR YOUR PREVIOUS KING CANDIDATE.

SWP

King Candidate Yodogawa

I AM KING CANDIDATE YODOGAWA.

PLEASE CALL ME YOTCHAN, EVERYONE ELSE DOES.
Yotchan?
DOESN'T MAKE MUCH OF AN IMPRES-SION...

LET'S SEE NOW...
SHFF
LET ME GET STRAIGHT TO THE POINT.

KOSUKE UEKI.

YOU ARE GOING TO QUIT THIS BATTLE...
SMILE
AREN'T YOU?

NO.
I'll keep fighting.
DADOOM
WHAT?!!

TAKA TAK
TAK TAKA TAK
TAKA TAK TAKA TAKA TAK
THAT'S STRANGE!! ACCORDING TO MY DATA...
...YOU WERE ENROLLED IN THIS TOURNAMENT WITHOUT KNOWING ANYTHING ABOUT IT, RIGHT?
AND HERE, LOOK! IN THE FIGHT AGAINST TAIRA, YOU GOT SERIOUS BURNS AND BRUISES!!
IN THE FIGHT AGAINST LI HO, YOU EVEN ENDED UP WITH SOME FRACTURES!

HAVEN'T YOU HAD ENOUGH?!
YOTCHAN, DO YOU WANT ME TO QUIT?
ULP
HUH?!!
I WON'T DO IT.

I'M GOING TO BE THIS TOURNAMENT'S CHAMPION.

I'VE MADE UP MY MIND.

Coffee

FWP

THAT'S WHY...

I MUST CONVINCE YOU TO QUIT!!

THE LAW OF UEKI

REMAINING TALENTS=11

HMM...
THIS LOOKS KIND OF FAMILIAR.

WHAT DO YOU MEAN KIND OF?
THESE ARE YOUR EXISTING TALENTS.
OH, I SEE.
IT'S THE LAW OF UEKI, ISN'T IT?

UEKI HAS 11 TALENTS LEFT, SO...
THE LAW OF UEKI
REMAINING TALENTS=11
HP
MAX
MP
MAX
HERE'S A QUESTION FOR YOU.
WHAT IS THE AVERAGE NUMBER OF TALENTS THAT THE OTHER CONTESTANTS HAVE?
I DUNNO!

ABOUT 160!!

!!?

NOW YOU SEE HOW MUCH OF A DISADVANTAGE UEKI HAS!!

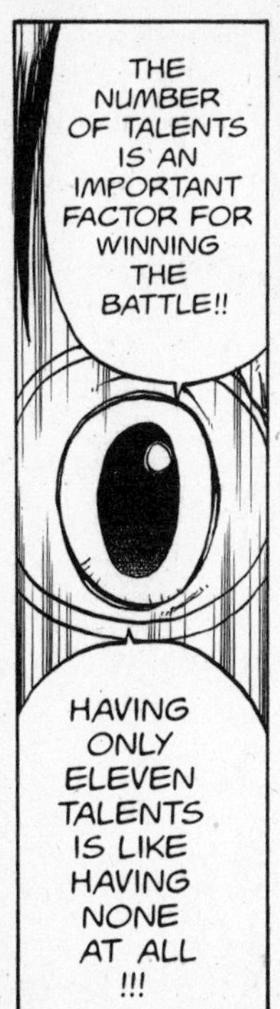

IT'S A MIRACLE YOU'VE SURVIVED THIS FAR!!

UEKI, YOU'VE GOT NO CHANCE OF WINNING!!

GNARRR
The tree devil and his minions headed for the town of humans!
The human hunt was about to begin.

ULP
...
THE HUMAN HUNT!!
Fukus Hibi
Tsubame Primary School Fukusuke Hibiki
The Brave Warrior and the Tree Devil

BUT WHERE THE HECK IS HE?
IN THE PICTURE BOOK, THE TREE DEVIL IS ALWAYS ATTRACTED TO STRIPES LIKE THESE, BUT...

GNARRR
DARN IT! I MUST EXPOSE THAT TREE DEVIL BEFORE...
HE STARTS THE HUMAN HUNT!!!

THERE'S NO WAY...

SLURP

THERE HE IS !!!

ALL RIGHT! I'LL SNEAK UP BEHIND HIM!!
TREE DEVIL, I'LL GET YOU...
Fukusuke Hibiki
DADOOM

PLASH
Fukusuke Hibiki
HEY !!
HUH ?

DEVIL ?
ZWOOP
DRIP DRIP
tea
HEY, BRAT...

YOU SAYING YOU KNOW OF OUR BOSS WELL ENOUGH TO KNOW HIS REPUTATION AS THE DEVIL OF FURIN, AND YOU STILL INSULTED HIM?
WELL ?!!
bam

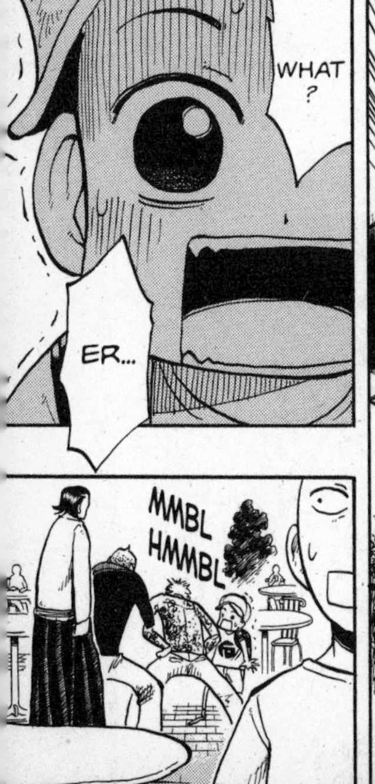
WHAT ?
ER...
MMBL HMMBL

NO WAY.
I WON'T QUIT.
I'll keep fighting.

DON'T YOU GET IT?
THERE'S NO WAY FOR YOU TO WIN THE BATTLE!
THE DATA IS CONCLU-SIVE!!
YOU NEVER KNOW UNLESS YOU TRY.
DADOOM

EVEN WORSE, YOU LOST THREE TALENTS BY HURTING PEOPLE WITH YOUR POWER!!
FRANTIC
LOSING TALENTS THE WAY YOU DO IS UNHEARD OF!!
LOST TALENTS
• Talent to be liked by girls
• Talent to study
• Talent to run

YOUR PREVIOUS KING CANDIDATE, KOBAYASHI, CONSIDERED THAT A SIGN OF HAVING A SENSE OF JUSTICE OR SOME NONSENSE LIKE THAT!
BUT IF THINGS CONTINUE THIS WAY, YOU'LL LOSE ALL YOUR TALENTS AND DISAPPEAR!!
HM?
TWITCH

NOW LOOK AT THIS!!
HUH?
FWP

WHAT'S THAT, YOTCHAN?
ER? This?

THE LATEST TECH-NOLOGY FROM THE CELESTIAL WORLD.
IT PROVIDES INFORMATION ABOUT TALENTS AND SUCH IN REAL-TIME.
REMAINING TALENTS=11
WOW.

WHACK SMACK SKRUKK
BLIP
BLIP
BLIP
REMAINING TALENTS=11
HMM?

HUH? THESE THREE DISAP-PEARED. Here.
OH YES, IT MEANS UEKI JUST LOST THREE MORE TALENTS.

...
WHAT?

© Fukusuke Hibiki

SLURP
coffee

WHAT ...?

WHAT ...!!

...?!!

REMAINING TALENTS=8
WHAT ...?!!

Chapter 26
It's 215 Against 8

HEY!
WHAT JUST HAPPENED ?!!
THE THREE MEN WHO WERE PICKING ON THAT KID ARE OUT COLD !!!

THAT BOY !!!
OH, UH... WE'RE JUST REHEARSING A PLAY !!
FOR OUR SCHOOL FESTIVAL ...!!
Is that all?
What a shock.
YUMMY.
WHAT'S THAT TREE ?!!
YOU, IDIOT !!
HMM ?
WHAT ARE YOU DOING, UEKI ?!!
IF YOU HURT PEOPLE WITH YOUR POWER...
SLAM
I LOSE MY TALENTS.
DADOOM
IF YOU KNOW THAT, THEN WHY THE HECK ...?!!

YOU JUST SAID YOU WANT TO WIN THE BATTLE !!
SO HOW CAN YOU JUST GO AND LOSE THREE OF YOUR TALENTS ?!
OOPS...

YOU ARE RIGHT.
DARN IT...

...
UEKI...
KlInk

I'LL BE MORE CAREFUL NEXT TIME !!
SLURP
DOINK
HOW CAN YOU BE SO CARE-FREE ?!!

UEKI.
HMM ?

NOW DO YOU UNDERSTAND?!! YOU'RE NOT SUITABLE FOR THIS BATTLE!!

TALENTS ARE THE KEY TO WINNING THE BATTLE AND YOU LOSE THEM WITHOUT A SECOND THOUGHT!

SEE? LET'S WITHDRAW!! SHALL WE? SHALL WE?!

Caffe La

YOTCHAN, IS THAT YOUR ADVICE AS A KING CANDIDATE?

YES, IT IS!!!

COME ON, UEKI!! LET'S WITH-DRAW...

HEY!!!

HUH?

TREE DEVIL !!!
YOU FINALLY DID IT !!!
Fukus Hibi

?
TREE DEVIL ?
BABUMP
BABUMP

WHAT DID I DO?
DON'T PRETEND YOU DON'T KNOW !!
THUMP
?

THE HUMAN HUNT !!
DADOOM
YOU FINALLY STARTED IT!!

WELL... I DID IT FOR YOUR SAKE...
SHUT UP, TREE DEVIL !!

BEEP
!!?
BEEP
BEEP
WHAT...
WHAT IS IT NOW ?!
BEEP
...
flip
?
THAT MEANS AN OPPONENT IS ABOUT TO APPEAR.
!!!
HE'S RIGHT OVER THERE!

WHAT...
AN ENEMY ?!!

YOU CAN USE THAT THING TO CHECK WHERE OPPONENTS ARE?!
It's not just for keeping track of talents?
IT ALSO SHOWS YOU WHAT KIND OF TALENTS YOU MIGHT ACQUIRE IF YOU DEFEAT A SPECIFIC OPPONENT.

BLIP
!

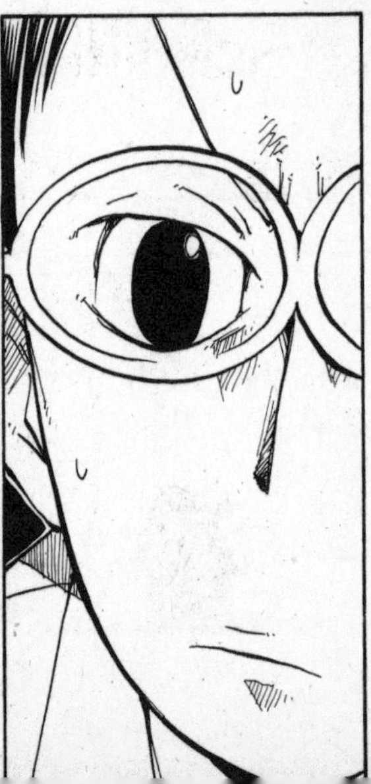

UEKI...
THIS IS THE DIRE SITUATION YOU ARE IN RIGHT NOW.

LOOK AT HOW MANY TALENTS YOUR NEXT OPPONENT HAS...

Bolo T

REMAINING TALENTS=215

TALENTS TO BE ACQUIRED BY DEFEATING

HE HAS 215!!!

REMAINING TALENTS=215

And this map shows where your opponent is now.
AND YOU'VE JUST LOST THREE...
SO YOU ONLY HAVE EIGHT!!
SO NOW DO YOU SEE?

IT WOULD BE FUTILE FOR YOU TO TAKE HIM ON.
BEEP BEEP...
I SEE... THAT'S WHERE HE IS.
HUH?

ALL RIGHT, I'M GOING TO WIN!
HUH ?!!
DASH
ACK
WAIT !!!

NO!
BEEP
BEEP
BEEP
UEKI IS ABOUT TO MEET THE ENEMY.

WHAT'S WITH THAT KID?!
ALL THE ODDS ARE AGAINST HIM. ANY NORMAL PERSON WOULD GIVE UP!!
TAK TAK TAK TAK TAK
HE ISN'T NORMAL!!
NOW THAT YOU'RE HIS KING CANDIDATE, YOU BETTER GET USED TO IT, YOTCHAN!!

THE OPPONENT HAS MORE THAN 200 TALENTS!!
UEKI WILL DEFINITELY LOSE TODAY...
NO HE WON'T!!
HUH?
DADUM
THAT KID FROM BEFORE!!

DON'T UNDER-ESTIMATE THE TREE DEVIL !!!

HE'S TRULY EVIL SO HE WON'T BE DEFEATED THAT EASILY !!!

YOU ARE HIS MINIONS, AND YOU DON'T EVEN KNOW THAT?

WHAT'S WITH ALL THIS TREE DEVIL BUSINESS?

DON'T PRETEND LIKE YOU DON'T KNOW!! HE'S ALREADY REVEALED HIMSELF AS THE TREE DEVIL!!

YOU'RE NOT MAKING MUCH SENSE...

IT'S ALL IN HERE !!!

The Brave Warrior and the Tree

Story & Art Robin Blossom the Third

Ha ha

OH DEAR! HE'S ENCOUN-TERED THE ENEMY...
THERE'S NO OTHER CHOICE NOW...

UEKI MUST LOSE...
...SO WE CAN DROP OUT OF THIS BATTLE AS SOON AS POSSIBLE.

I TOLD YOU, THE SNEAKY TREE DEVIL WON'T BE DEFEATED SO EASILY!!
...
I'M SORRY !!

PHEW

THERE YOU ARE !!

KOSUKE UEKI.
WITH EIGHT TALENTS.
THE TALENT I CAN GET BY DEFEATING HIM IS THE TALENT TO LOOK AHEAD!
YEAH... IT'S ALL HERE.

MY NAME IS BOLO...
HEY!
?

YOU'LL MAKE FOR GOOD PREY!!
ZLIKT
YOU'RE AN EASY MARK AND I'LL GET THE TALENT TO LOOK AHEAD!!
ZLIKT

STOP ALL THIS TALKING...
...AND LET'S GET TO FIGHTING.
!!

FOOSH
!!
YOU'RE AN IRRITATING LITTLE RUNT!

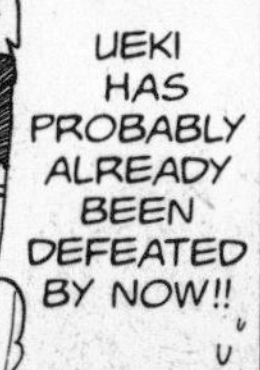
UEKI HAS PROBABLY ALREADY BEEN DEFEATED BY NOW!!

TAK TAK TAK TAK TAK
......
NO WAY!!!

UEKI ?!!
!!!

THUD!
AH!!
The tree devil down?!!

FWAP
!
I TOLD YOU!

HE HAD NO CHANCE OF WINNING...
AT LEAST NOW I CAN GO BACK TO THE CELESTIAL WORLD.

WAIT !!
LOOK !!!

!!!

hmph
!!
THAT SMARTS.
SEE!! THE TREE DEVIL IS HARD TO KILL!! I told you, didn't I!!!
HEH HEH.
IMPOSSI-BLE...

IT'S LIKE I SAID!
IMPOS-SIBLE...

HOW COULD THIS BE?! I'VE GOT 215 TALENTS AND HE'S ONLY GOT EIGHT...

THE LITTLE RUNT!!!
SWIP

Chapter 27
Yotchan's True Identity

FWOOOSH

WOW.
YOU ARE THE FIRST TO EVER SURVIVE MY INITIAL ASSAULT AND ATTACK BACK!
!!

SEE?! THE TREE DEVIL IS NOT EASY PREY!!
Heh-heh
IMPOS-SIBLE!!

KOSUKE UEKI HAS ONLY EIGHT TALENTS!
HE'S PITTED AGAINST BOLO T WHO HAS 215!!!
I WAS SURE THIS BATTLE WOULD HAVE BEEN OVER ALREADY...

DAD
?!!
WHAT ARE YOU DOING HERE?
!!

FUKUSUKE
?

LET'S GO HOME AND EAT!
NO!! THE TREE DEVIL IS FIGHTING... !!!
drag drag
I'LL READ YOU A PICTURE BOOK WHEN WE GET HOME.
NO, THE TREE DEVIL IS HERE !!!

No, the tree devil! The tree devil!
Hmm...
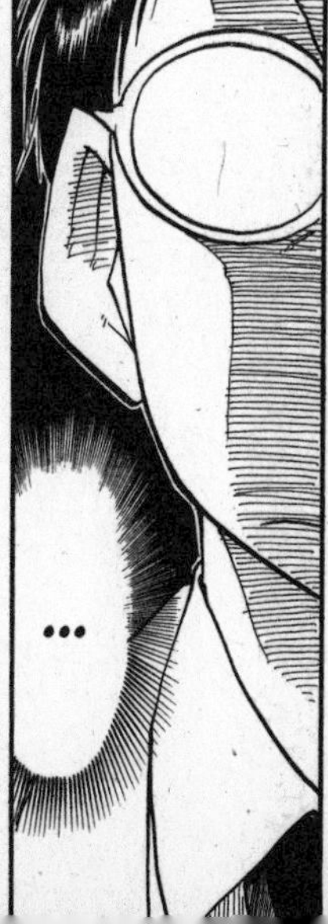
...

HA HA!! YOUR PREVIOUS COUNTER-ATTACK WAS JUST A FLUKE, WASN'T IT?
THIS TIME I'LL BREAK YOUR SKULL IN TWO...
SWP

WITH THE POWER TO CHANGE MY HEAD INTO DIAMONDS!!!
FZZZZZ
!!!!
DIA...
VROOOOSSH
DIAMONDS?!!
SO THAT'S YOUR POWER.
I WON'T GET HIT BY YOU AGAIN.

FSSHA
KRAKK
KRAKK
GRKK
GRKK
GRKK
!!!?

COM-
PARED
TO
DIAMONDS,
TREES
ARE...
...LIKE
BUTTER.

!!!

SKREEE
UEKI !!

HEY, MORI.
FOOP
WHAT ARE YOU DOING HERE ...?
SPLUT
SPLUT
SPLUT
DID YOU JUST NOTICE ?!!

TSK.
MUTTER
IT LOOKS LIKE HE DIDN'T TAKE MUCH DAMAGE...

DID YOU SAY SOMETHING, YOTCHAN?
?
NO, NO, NO !!!

Hey! You're covered in blood!!
Whoa, you're right.
...

IT SEEMS THAT HE UNCONSCIOUSLY UTILIZED HIS TALENT TO USE INSTANT REFLEXES TO AVOID SERIOUS INJURY.
SWISH SWISH
IT'D BE SO MUCH EASIER IF HE LOST QUICKLY...

ACTUALLY...

I HAVE TO MAKE SURE THAT UEKI LOSES !!

YOU PROBABLY HAVEN'T REALIZED IT YET, BUT...

...YOUR ARCH-ENEMY...

ROBERT HAYDN...

...IS STILL ALIVE !!!

ROBERT'S KING CANDIDATE MARGARET!!!

THE CELESTIAL WITH THE BEST CHANCE OF GETTING THE THRONE...

CRAP!

YOU TOOK MY ATTACK TWICE AND YOU'RE STILL STANDING? YOU HURT MY PRIDE...

...I WON'T !!

DASH

SWP

DODGE !

IT'S NO USE.

BLIP

YOU SEE...

Law of Bolo

BOLO HAS THE TALENT TO CAPTURE !!!

GRAB

ACK !?!

SWUK

...TILES !!!

!!!

UGH !!
WELL, WELL...
LIKE I THOUGHT, THIS IS THE BEST HE CAN DO WITH JUST EIGHT TALENTS.

PLEASE JUST GIVE UP, UEKI!
FOR MY SAKE! SO I CAN BECOME KING'S AIDE!!

HA HA HA! I HAVE 215 TALENTS!
IF I FULLY UTILIZE ALL OF THEM, I CAN WIN WITHOUT EVEN USING MY POWER!!
USE ALL YOUR...
...TALENTS ?

FOR EXAMPLE...
THE TALENT TO KICK ROCKS.
Law of Bolo
CLONK
THE TALENT TO WRAP AROUND...
ZOOP
!
OOF!

DIAMOND HEADBUTT !!!
SWUKK
YAAG !!
!!!
OOPS !
I USED MY POWER. ♡
IT SEEMS...
...THAT THIS FIGHT WILL BE OVER SOON.
HEY...
WHAT'S UP WITH THIS GUY!! DOESN'T HIS POWER HAVE A LIMITATION ?!!
UEKI CAN ONLY TRANSFORM THE TRASH HE CAN HOLD IN HIS HANDS!!
ALL POWERS HAVE A LIMITATION.
BUT THE MOBILE DEVICE DOES NOT GIVE US INFORMATION ABOUT THE OPPONENTS' POWERS.

EVEN IF IT DID...
...UEKI'S GOT NO CHANCE OF DEFEATING AN OPPONENT WITH OVER 200 TALENTS!
NNGH
FINE...

IN THAT CASE...
I'LL USE ALL MY TALENTS TOO.
?!!

TALENT TO DANCE! TALENT TO DANCE! TALENT TO DANCE!
twirl twirl
SLAPITY SLAP SLAP
TALENT TO DANCE !!!
TALENT TO SWIM! TALENT TO SWIM! TALENT TO SWIM!
SHKSHH SHKSHH
SLAPITY SLAP
SLAP
SLAP
TALENT TO SWIM!!
HE'S NOT KIDDING.

AND NOW...
THE TALENT TO...
FSSHA
HIT A TARGET!
!!!
WHAT... ?!!!
FWATHOOM
OOF !!
RIIPP
RIIPP

...
HMPH!!
HA HA HA!! SO MUCH FOR YOUR SO-CALLED TALENT TO HIT A TARGET!!!
DASH
HUFF HUFF HUFF
YOU CAN'T EVEN PROPERLY USE YOUR MEASLY EIGHT TALENTS!!
HEY, BY THE WAY, WHAT IS THE LIMITATION OF YOUR POWER?
HUFF HUFF HUFF
HA HA!!
I'LL TELL YOU AS A GIFT YOU CAN TAKE TO YOUR GRAVE!!
I CAN ONLY CHANGE MY HEAD INTO DIAMONDS WHEN I PUT MY HANDS IN MY POCKETS!!
THOUGHT SO.

THEN WITHOUT POCKETS...

ZOOP

...YOU CAN'T USE YOUR POWER.

HA HA!!

WHAT ARE YOU TALKING ABOUT?

SHFF

...

WHAT...

TORN

WHAT?!!

DA

WITHOUT POCKETS...

SH

YOU CAN'T USE YOUR POWER TO CHANGE YOUR HEAD INTO DIAMONDS.
!!!

TORN

!

IF YOUR HEAD IS NOT A DIAMOND...
...THEN IT WON'T HURT AS MUCH THIS TIME ROUND !!!

Chapter 28 Head to Head!

Chapter 28
Head to Head!
!!!

Coloring Page
Color it in as you like.

NOT...

...POS-
SIBLE...

THUD

!!!

DADOOM

HEY, THAT STILL HURT!

!!!

!!!

WHEN DID HE DO THAT TO MY POCKETS?!

!
THIS IS BAD !!
HUFF HUFF

BOLO T RECEIVED SERIOUS DAMAGE FROM THAT ATTACK!!
HIS POWER TO CHANGE HIS HEAD INTO DIAMONDS IS VITAL...
BOLO T.

THE POWER IS MEANT TO PROTECT HIS HEAD BECAUSE IT'S HIS WEAK SPOT!!
IF HE RECEIVES ANOTHER HEADBUTT...

BOLO T WILL BE OUT OF THE GAME !!!
HUFF
HUFF
HUFF
Hmph...
I TOLD YOU I HAVE 215 TALENTS, DIDN'T I?!

IF MY POCKETS ARE TORN...
FPP
FPP

I CAN MEND THEM...
!!!
FWIP
SWP
SRUSH
SHH
TA
...IN NO TIME AT ALL...
DAA
...WITH THE TALENT TO SEW !!!

WHO CARES! IF YOU TEAR MY POCKETS, IT WON'T MAKE A DIFFER-ENCE!!!

HMPH!

GOOD!!

NOW UEKI HAS NO CHANCE OF WINNING AT ALL!!

WITH MY SEWING, I CAN USE MY POWER AS MANY TIMES AS I LIKE!!!

DASH

SWI
KK
UGH!
OOF!!!
FSSHAAA
T
UP
YAAAAAH!!
SWP
FWATHOOM
!
RIIPP
RIIPP
MY POCKETS AGAIN ?!

!?
I CAN FIX THEM NO MATTER HOW MANY TIMES YOU TEAR THEM!!
SFRSH
IT'S NO USE !!
DONE

FWSH
I KNOW !
!!!
GRAB
UMF !!
WHSSH
HMF.

VROO
STOP RUNNING AROUND !!
WITH THIS DIAMOND HEADBUTT, I'LL SQUASH YOU LIKE A LITTLE BUG...
OOSSH

...INSTANTLY...

SH

FF

?

HUH !!!

FSHOO OOM

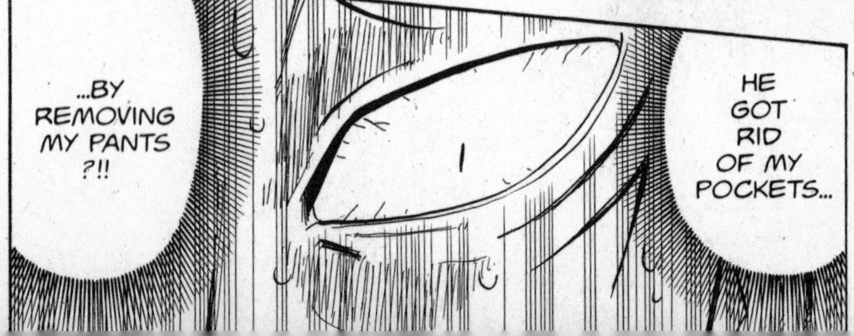

KLUD
TEARING OFF THE POCKETS DIDN'T WORK...
SO I HAD NO CHOICE BUT TO COMPLETELY PANTS YOU.

DADOOM
I WIN!
!!!

NOT...
Ueki!!
NOT...
BEEP BEEP

NOT POSSIBLE!!
THE LAW OF UEKI
TALENT TO DRESS STYLISH ACQUIRED.
REMAINING TALENTS=9

BOLO T HAD 215 TALENTS!!!
HOW IS IT POSSIBLE THAT UEKI WON?!!

IT CAN'T BE TRUE...
THERE MUST BE SOME SORT OF MISTAKE !!!

FIRST AID!
Trousers
With that ?
SHRSH

...
UEKI, IT WAS A FLUKE THAT YOU WON THIS TIME, BUT...
LET'S QUIT NOW.
SIGH
THERE'S NO POINT OF CONTINUING ANYMORE...
WHY ARE YOU STILL SAYING THAT ?!

OH, NEVER MIND!! NO MATTER WHAT HAPPENS, THERE IS NO WAY FOR UEKI TO WIN THIS TOURNAMENT!!

THE WINNER CAN ONLY BE ROBERT HAYDN...

...

HOLD ON...

IS...
...THAT GUY...
...STILL ALIVE?

THAT WAY...

...I CAN AVENGE MR. K !!!

...
YAHHH
AND THEN I'LL WIN THE TOURNAMENT.

...
GONG
WHAT... ?!!

THERE IS NO WAY FOR YOU TO BEAT HIM!! HE'S THE STRONGEST COMPETITOR !!
HE'S ROBERT HAYDN !!!
HE'S ROBERT HAYDN !!!
UEKI...!!

OH!

WHAT ABOUT THAT KID?
IS HE ALL RIGHT? HE WAS DRAGGED AWAY BY HIS FATHER...

NO!!
PLEASE STOP, DAD!!!

YES, YES!! GOOD, YOU'RE SO COOL, FUKU-SUKE!!
FAASSH FAASSH
YOU'RE THE BEST!! GOOD! GOOD!
PLEASE FIND ANOTHER SUBJECT FOR YOUR CONTEST!!

DON'T WORRY!! YOUR DAD IS A PROFES-SIONAL PHOTO-GRAPHER!!
DADDY IS NOT ASHAMED OF YOU!!!
I'M THE ONE WHO'S ASHAMED!!!

DAD, I HAVE NO TIME FOR THIS!!
THE TREE DEVIL HAS ALREADY STARTED HIS HUMAN HUNT!!
The Brave Warrior and the Tree Devil

!!
FUKU-SUKE...

YOU WILL BE DEFEATED!!

PHEW, I'M EXHAUSTED.

End of Volume 3

Bonus Seiichiro and the Old Dude

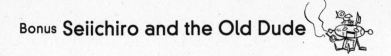

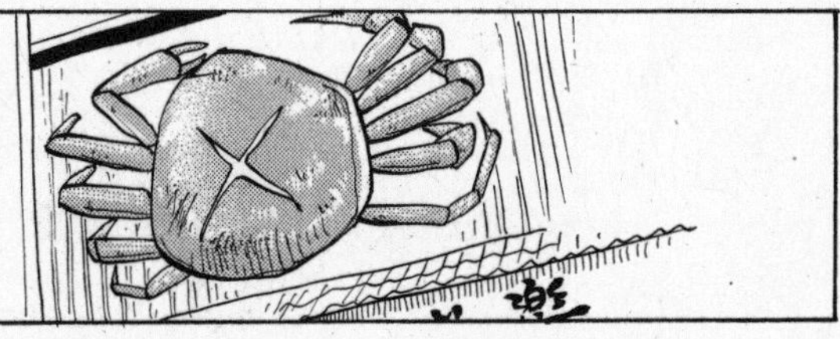

Osaka

MY NAME IS SEIICHIRO SANO.
SHUF
SHUF
Wonder how Ueki is doing?
MY DREAM IS TO GET THE TALENT TO DIG AND HAVE MY OWN HOT SPRING SPA.

HEY, YOU OVER THERE!
HUH?

GRRRR

HELP!
Chew
Chew
Chew
I'M REALLY SCARED OF DOGS.
SWING
SWING

HARD TO BELIEVE, ISN'T IT?
IT'S THE SAD TRUTH THOUGH.
SHLORP
AND MY OIL IS LEAKING.
IS THAT SO?
WHO THE HECK ARE YOU?

◆ IN THE END, SANO HAD TO FIND A HOT SPRING ON HIS OWN.

My hair gets in the way ...

Tsubasa Fukuchi

When I get a haircut, I always have a difficult time deciding how to get it cut. I agonize over it. I really agonize over it. I think about it and think about it and then I end up saying, "Give me the usual."

DIFFERENT LAWS 3